To Brett and Bryce

Always "Have Heart."
Best Wishes!

David Eckstein

Have Heart

By David Eckstein

with Greg Brown

Published by Positively For Kids, Inc.
20912 33rd Ave SE
Bothell, WA 98021   1.800.600.KIDS
www.PositivelyForKids.com

Printed in the United States of America.

This book is dedicated to

MILLER CHILDREN'S HOSPITAL

AT
LONG BEACH
MEMORIAL MEDICAL CENTER

MemorialCare®

✚ MEMORIALCARE®
THE STANDARD OF EXCELLENCE IN HEALTH CARE

Children from all over the Southern California area depend on Miller Children's Hospital to get well. For babies and toddlers to teens and young adults, Miller Children's Hospital is a special place where caring professionals are devoted to the health and well-being of children.

To the patients at Miller Children's Hospital, we hope this book inspires you to always reach for your dreams — even when they seem out of grasp. Believe in yourselves, and dreams really can come true!

And to the physicians, nurses, therapists, staff and volunteers at Miller Children's Hospital, thank you for your work with the patients and helping make their dreams possible. You are Angels!

Miller Children's Hospital is part of the MemorialCare Medical Centers of Southern California, the official hospitals of the Anaheim Angels. Other MemorialCare Medical Centers include Anaheim Memorial, Long Beach Memorial, Orange Coast Memorial (Fountain Valley) and Saddleback Memorial (Laguna Hills).

Harry How/Getty Images

My name is David Eckstein and you could call me a short shortstop. Ever since I picked up a bat, I've been the shortest player on the field in most games I've played. I stand just 5-foot, 6¾ inches. Some little leaguers are taller than me.

Some baseball people said I'd never play in the Major Leagues. Some even said it to my face. I don't have all five talents that scouts seek — hitting for average, hitting with power, speed, fielding, and arm strength. It's true, my swing isn't picture perfect. I don't hit many home runs. I'm not the fastest on the field, and my arm is just strong enough.

However, I always had the desire to be the best baseball player I could be since I was old enough to hold a bat. I never gave up, and I never lost heart. As a result, not only did I become a Major League baseball player, but I played a role in helping the 2002 Anaheim Angels win their first World Series® Championship.

Sometimes people tell me that I'm like the children's story about *The Little Engine that Could*. I just kept trying and believing I could — having heart. Someone's heart cannot be measured in inches, statistics, or seconds. Still, ordinary people who have heart do amazing things and beat the odds.

AP/Wide World Photos

What do I mean by having heart?

A perfect example of a team having heart can be seen on the 2002 team produced video: A Red Dawn Rises. Disney's movie makers could not have written such an incredible tale as the 2002 season of the Anaheim Angels.

The experts, armed with statistics, never expected us to win the 2002 World Series®. The year before we were 41 games out of first place. History was against us as the Angels had never been to the World Series®. Also, a 6-14 start ranked as the team's worst ever.

And yet, somehow, the team's day-by-day actions turned into a magical championship script. Our team showed heart in courage, effort, perseverance, selflessness, and a never say lose attitude.

AP/Wide World Photos

The seven games of the World Series® proved to be the culmination of our dramatic season. In the seventh inning of Game 6, we were down 5-0 to the San Francisco Giants. A historic rally kept us alive for the deciding Game 7.

Southern California celebrated our victory with three wonderful parades. We received our World Series® rings before the second game of the 2003 season, and I gave my ring to my dad. Although I would like to earn more World Series® rings, I do not play for rings or trophies.

Why do I play? Why do I love baseball? Why do I hustle so much? Why do I risk injury? Why do I practice so much in the offseason? To understand what's in my heart, you have to understand my family.

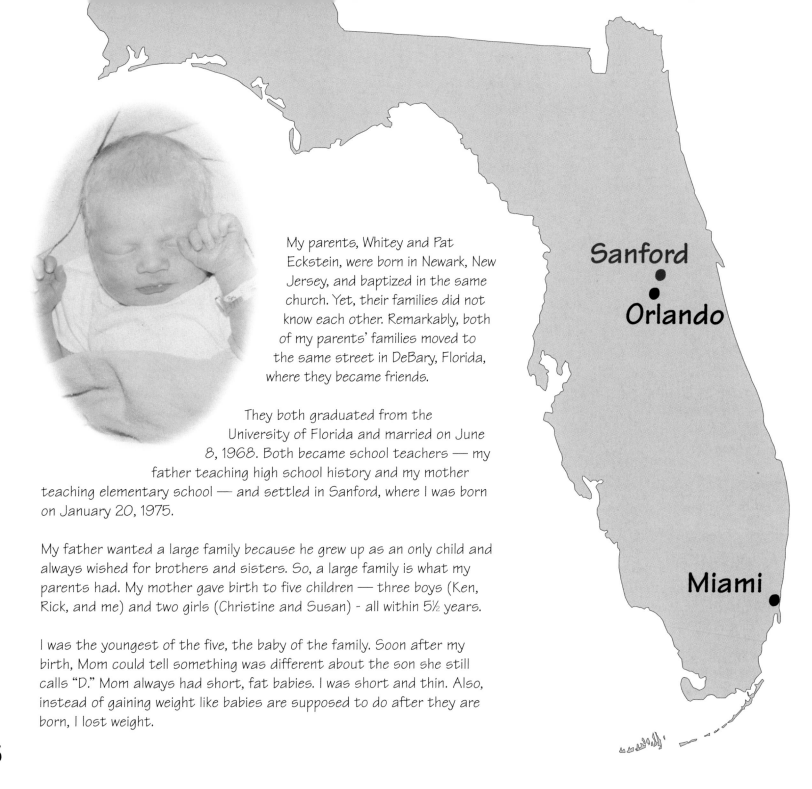

My parents, Whitey and Pat Eckstein, were born in Newark, New Jersey, and baptized in the same church. Yet, their families did not know each other. Remarkably, both of my parents' families moved to the same street in DeBary, Florida, where they became friends.

They both graduated from the University of Florida and married on June 8, 1968. Both became school teachers — my father teaching high school history and my mother teaching elementary school — and settled in Sanford, where I was born on January 20, 1975.

My father wanted a large family because he grew up as an only child and always wished for brothers and sisters. So, a large family is what my parents had. My mother gave birth to five children — three boys (Ken, Rick, and me) and two girls (Christine and Susan) - all within 5½ years.

I was the youngest of the five, the baby of the family. Soon after my birth, Mom could tell something was different about the son she still calls "D." Mom always had short, fat babies. I was short and thin. Also, instead of gaining weight like babies are supposed to do after they are born, I lost weight.

Sanford

Orlando

Miami

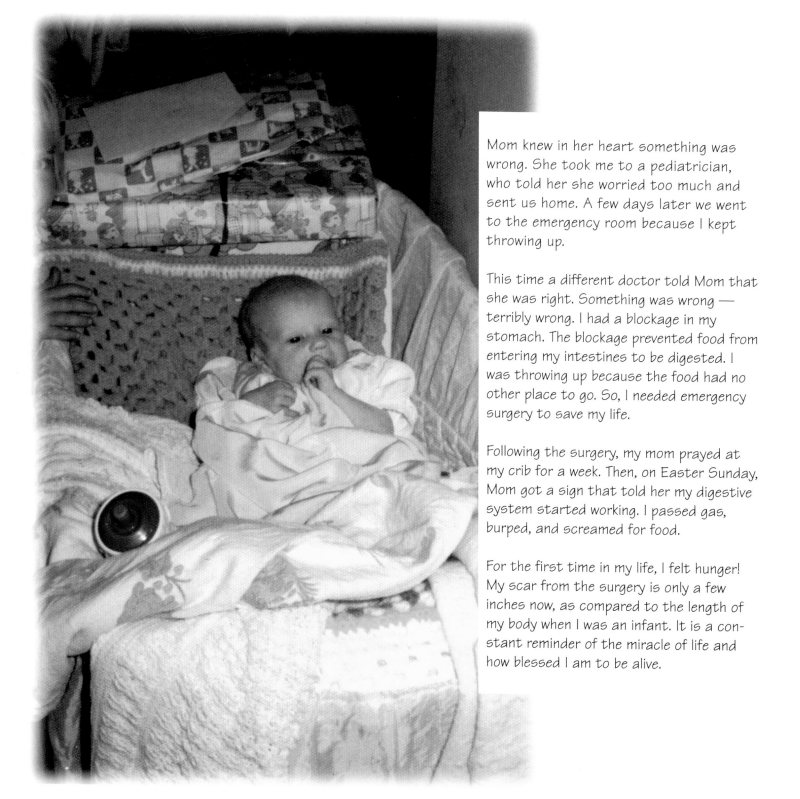

Mom knew in her heart something was wrong. She took me to a pediatrician, who told her she worried too much and sent us home. A few days later we went to the emergency room because I kept throwing up.

This time a different doctor told Mom that she was right. Something was wrong — terribly wrong. I had a blockage in my stomach. The blockage prevented food from entering my intestines to be digested. I was throwing up because the food had no other place to go. So, I needed emergency surgery to save my life.

Following the surgery, my mom prayed at my crib for a week. Then, on Easter Sunday, Mom got a sign that told her my digestive system started working. I passed gas, burped, and screamed for food.

For the first time in my life, I felt hunger! My scar from the surgery is only a few inches now, as compared to the length of my body when I was an infant. It is a constant reminder of the miracle of life and how blessed I am to be alive.

7

My parents will tell you I was born loving baseball. As a two-year-old, I'd sit and watch a whole game on television, barely moving a muscle. By age three, I knew the names of players.

At age four, I could remember entire team rosters. My dad loved watching the Atlanta Braves games on TV, and so did I. My family's favorite player was Dale Murphy, who to this day I consider to be a great baseball player as well as a great person. In 1979, my family and I had the opportunity to see Dale Murphy play when we went to Atlanta on a family vacation.

We didn't go on many family vacations. Besides not having much extra money, my parents said if one member of our family couldn't go on vacation, nobody would.

Fortunately, sandy, warm beaches were close by. I loved to boogie board; I didn't enjoy getting stung by jellyfish, though. An Eckstein beach tradition is to have family races between the lifeguard stands.

Another memorable family trip for me was when we traveled north to Cooperstown, New York, to see the Baseball Hall of Fame. I was five years old. I can still remember having my picture taken in front of Mickey Mantle's display and hitting in the batting cages.

I was in awe with the whole experience, so you can imagine how honored and thrilled I was when the Baseball Hall of Fame asked me for my cleats last year.

From Cooperstown, my family traveled to New York City and watched a game in Yankee Stadium. We were in the upper deck near the left-field line. What impressed me the most about the game was seeing Yankee Manager Billy Martin come out and argue a call. Because of this trip, I knew that baseball was what I wanted to do more than anything else in the world.

My family lived in a modest four-bedroom house in Sanford, which is about 35 miles from the Walt Disney World® Resort. It was always a very special day to go to Walt Disney World Resort. However, Walt Disney World Resort was at best a once-a-year treat, so my backyard was my amusement park.

I first started playing baseball in our backyard with my brother, Rick, as my coach.

We always practiced catching. We even practiced in the house playing catch with a tennis ball from bed to bed. To practice hitting, Rick and I played "challenge rounds" in the backyard with either tennis balls or racquetballs. We would stand approximately 20 feet from each other and the pitcher would throw the ball as hard as he could trying to strike out the batter.

Rick and I show off our catch during my first fishing trip. On a different day, Dad took us out in a boat and I remember alligators swam all around us. Gators and snakes scared me the most as a kid.

For fielding, we belted hot grounders to each other from the same 20-foot distance. Because our back-yard was not the size of a little league baseball field, we made special ground rules. If we hit it in a certain area, it was a double. If we hit it in another area, it was a grand slam. We never wanted to hit a home run over the left-field fence because on the other side was a two-lane road with traffic. Plus, it was a good way to lose the ball.

As we grew older, Rick and I played baseball with friends in the neighborhood. Although the guys were at least two years older than me, I would still tag along and play with the older kids. I knew that in order to keep up with the older guys I had to push myself. So right from the start I was the little guy trying to prove himself.

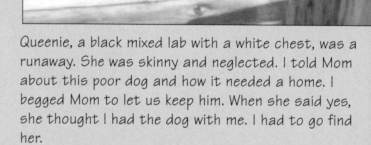

I have a soft heart for animals, especially dogs. I've always enjoyed being around animals and having pets.

The backyard at my parents' house is a pet cemetery. We didn't put gravestone markers in the dirt, but buried there are five family dogs — Lady, Ruby, Rusty, Pete, and Queenie, — 13 puppies which didn't survive birth, a guinea pig (Coffee), three cockatiels (Baby, Katie, and Huncey) and a cat named Francis.

We always had pets around our house. We gave our pets love and respect. They were part of our family.

Rusty, an English springer, grew up with me and died just a few years ago of old age. A piece of my childhood died with him.

Queenie, a black mixed lab with a white chest, was a runaway. She was skinny and neglected. I told Mom about this poor dog and how it needed a home. I begged Mom to let us keep him. When she said yes, she thought I had the dog with me. I had to go find her.

Ruby gave us a scare during the only Hurricane that damaged our house. Hurricane "David" hit Florida in 1980. It knocked down our fence and Ruby ran away. A few days later she came home and gave birth to 15 puppies. Only two survived, Tippy and Duke.

The summer before first grade I got my chance to play tee ball. When coaches handed out our mustard-yellow uniforms, I rushed to a restroom to put it on.

Mom says my face lit up with excitement. My pants were on backwards, my jersey was but-toned unevenly and hanging out, and my hat was on crooked. Mom wished she had taken a picture. I promptly ran through a puddle and splattered the uniform with mud. I was ready to play my first "real" game!

The next season mom did not want me to play tee ball again because she felt I was too advanced for it. Rick's Pony baseball coach, Coach Suggs, agreed and let me serve as the batboy for his Mustang team.

I took it seriously and hustled from the dugout to the plate to pick up the bats. I watched every play and soaked in all the details of the game. Best of all, I got to practice with the older team and my brother Rick.

My relationship with Rick and the rest of my family emphasizes the foremost rule in the Eckstein household: "family first."

My father would always say:

> "Family is the most important thing."

> "You can always depend on family."

> "We do not do anything unless it is as a family."

This meant that I spent a lot of time playing together with my brothers and sisters, sharing a room with my brothers, and going everywhere as a family.

Ecksteins' rules of the house

- Mind our parents.
- Family comes first.
- Everyone shares.
- Be respectful of all adults; address adults "Yes, Sir" or Yes, Ma'am."
- No talking back.
- Say your prayers every day and go to church on Sundays.
- Give 100 percent in whatever you do.
- No pouting or complaining.

My parents were always home with us when they were not at work. Many Friday nights, particularly during Lent, we had cheese pizza from our favorite pizza place and would watch "Happy Days" as a family.

On Saturdays, we all would go to the mall to play video games while Mom and Dad watched. Afterward, we'd go to Steak 'n Shake for dinner. I remember these times not because anything extraordinary happened, but because how happy I felt just doing ordinary things with the family. So, although I did not grow up rich in money, I grew up rich in values.

When it came to food, we were never forced to eat something we didn't like. Mom often made three different meals as we had different favorites. A taste I hate to this day is ketchup. I eat hamburgers plain.

Believe it or not, our family played well together. We had a pool table. We'd put on family plays. We played "The Price Is Right," using pillows for curtains. And we had silly competitions — who could hold themselves up the longest with one hand on a dresser and the other on a bed post with feet dangling.

Ken and my sisters didn't play team sports. They took some gymnastics classes but never competed. Ken competed in public speaking and had top grades. My sisters excelled in the classroom as well. They all were class presidents. Rick and I followed in their footsteps to be class presidents, too.

We did play golf together. Dad would give family clinics. A golf club sent me back to the hospital when I was about 2½.

Rick was practicing in our front yard. I walked into his swing and got clubbed in the head. Oh, did I bleed. My blond hair turned ketchup red. Mom rushed me to the emergency room. When she saw the doctor stitching my wound, she passed out. I came home giggling.

17

Happy Acres Kindergarten and Child Care in Sanford, Florida. I was four years old. That's me in the first row, wearing the yellow shirt.

When it came to school, there was no arguing about the importance of education. With both of my parents being teachers, there were no excuses for poor study habits or bad grades. My parents usually knew my grades before I did.

I knew that if there ever was a problem, my dad had no problem marching right into my classroom and discussing the problem in front of the entire class. Fortunately for me, I enjoyed going to school and did well.

My handwriting is what gave me a little trouble in school. Everyone in my family has perfect handwriting except me. Compared to them, mine is sloppy. Mom always called it chicken scratch.

Whenever my family hears someone comment about how neat my autograph looks, we all look at each other and smile.

In fifth grade, I was selected from my class as the recipient of Disney's Dreamers and Doers award. I was invited to Walt Disney World Resort to meet Mickey Mouse and receive my award.

Being one of the shortest people in my class was not a problem. All of my older brothers and sisters were short so they experienced all the "short jokes" before me.

We all learned to laugh along rather than get upset. In fact, my brother Ken used his shortness to his advantage by being elected president of his ninth grade class with the slogan "4-foot-9 vote Eckstein."

I learned a person's size does not determine what they can accomplish. What counts is the size of a person's heart — the attitude on the inside to be their best — that is the true measure of a person.

Things I don't do well

- Handwriting
- Singing
- Public speaking
- Anything mechanical

During my little league days I played shortstop and second base. At age 12, a new coach moved me to third and even center field for a short time. I didn't question it because I did not care where I played, just as long as I played. Eventually, I was moved back to second and that is the position I played throughout high school and college.

The whole family got involved with our baseball games — except Dad. Mom helped keep score and Ken, Christine, and Susan cheered from the stands. But Dad stayed home.

Why? Because he wanted youth baseball to be fun for us. He didn't want to rob our joy by taking it too seriously. Believe me, not one thing that happens in youth baseball will determine if someone makes it to the Major Leagues.

Can you find me in this picture? I'm in the front row, second from the right.

Dad was interested. After every game, Rick and I would tell him about it, replaying our at-bats pitch by pitch. Dad did sneak in to watch playoff and All-Star games. He watched all my high school games.

Courtesy of Tommy Vincent/Seminole Herald

Courtesy of Tommy Vincent/Seminole Herald

I experienced my first "World Series®" when I was in high school. Our Seminole Pony baseball team made it to the Colt World Series® for 15 and 16 year olds in Lafayette, Indiana.

We were knocked out in the first round. I remember teammates crying when we lost our final game. I didn't cry. I play the game to the best of my ability. I learn from my mistakes and move on.

For me, there were no tears, but determination to learn and to move forward. When I did cry, I cried over something completely different.

When I was in the seventh grade, life changed dramatically. My sister, Susan, who was 16 at the time, looked run-down. She just wasn't acting like herself. Mom felt in her heart that something was wrong. Mom took Susan to the doctor for a checkup. They discovered that her kidneys had failed.

Kidneys, located in the lower back, are needed to clean the blood in our bodies. She was rushed in an ambulance to Shands Hospital in Gainesville, Florida, which is about 100 miles away. For 11 months, Susan fought for her life. She did dialysis to clean her blood. She needed a kidney transplant. Mom was a perfect match, so she gave Susan one of her kidneys on November 29, 1988.

On December 16th, Susan and Mom were finally released from the hospital. Everyone was thankful. The long ordeal seemed to be over. However, as Mom and Susan arrived home, the phone rang.

It was Susan's doctor. Mom asked, "What's wrong with Susan now?" He replied, "It's not Susan, it's Christine."

The Ecksteins go to Washington: (from left) Mom, Rick, Dad, Ken, Me, Christine, and Susan.

Lab tests showed that Christine was in kidney failure, and she needed to start dialysis as soon as possible. The news seemed almost unbelievable. Just when we thought we had gotten our lives back, we were starting all over again. This was a time I remember crying.

Ten months later, my brother Ken began dialysis as well. Despite our family misfortune, nobody blamed God or turned bitter or asked: "Why us?"

Our faith taught us things happen for a reason. We might not know what that reason is, but our job is to move forward - taking it one day at a time and doing the best we can.

Ken, Christine, and Susan did dialysis four times a day, yet Ken needed more. He was hooked up to a machine for 10 hours a day. I can remember watching as they bravely went on with their lives never using their condition as an excuse. In fact, they all continued with their schooling. During his dialysis, Ken went to Washington, D.C., to serve as a Congressional intern. As a high school junior, he served as a Congressional page. He was voted "Page of the Year." We all were so proud of him. We took a family trip to visit him.

After waiting two years, Christine and Ken received successful transplants only four days apart from different donors in July of 1991. What a miracle of life it was. All of the transplants were successful. Thankfully, neither Rick nor I have kidney problems.

Living through this difficult time solidified our family ties. It also made us stronger and more determined to live our lives to the fullest.

Ken, Christine, and Susan met an interesting friend during their hospital treatments. Richard Sawyer grew up with many ailments. Hospitals were his second home. He had undergone three kidney transplants when Ken first met him. Despite his health problems, he took on life with courage and humor. Ken, Christine, Susan, and Richard would joke around saying whoever died first would come back to watch over the others. Unfortunately, Richard passed first. He died on the operating table during a liver transplant.

23

By the time I reached high school, things were almost normal in our house. School and baseball were my focus. I lived a pretty boring life. I didn't smoke or drink alcohol and didn't go to parties. I had a circle of close friends and we did things together.

My dad always said, "Show me a man's friends and I'll show you the man." One of my close friends then, and now, is Terry Tillis, a captain in the U.S. Army. He fought in Iraq, serving in the 4th Infantry out of Fort Hood, Texas.

He once gave me a birthday card that said, "Sorry I couldn't buy you anything because I am down to my last dollar." Inside the card was a dollar bill. The gesture exemplified not only Terry's incredible giving nature, but also his great sense of humor as well. Terry also helped me become a better fielder by smashing tennis balls at my feet from close range with a tennis racket.

On my 16th birthday, Dad gave me a great gift — my most embarrassing moment in high school. He came into my Latin class and sang, "Happy Birthday." Then he sang "Sweet Sixteen and Has Never Been Kissed." Despite my embarrassment at the time, I look back on this memory warmly, remembering how special my dad tried to make me feel. When I become a father, I might end up doing the same thing.

Eckstein's hustle helps Seminole to title

☐ The junior second baseman went 4-for-9 with an inside-the-park homer in the state tourney.

By Jill Cousins
OF THE SENTINEL STAFF

ATHLETE OF THE WEEK

David Eckstein has a difficult time describing his love for baseball. But when he takes the field, his exuberance tells the story.

Eckstein, Seminole's ___ second baseman, ___ nnings. He ___ ld position, ___ ut after the ___ s a one-man ___ mmates with

___ ep talk to Da- ___ all the time," ___ s said. "He gets ___ game. He really ___ up when they're ___ ren't down many ___ gives 100 percent

photos: I-16

___ re. ___ within. He's that type

Photo by Mindy Schauer/Sentinel

During high school, and even today, I try to make my parents proud of me. If you are faced with a decision, and you don't know what's right or wrong, ask yourself this: "Will my choice make my parents proud of me?" If the answer is yes, that's almost always the right choice.

The highlight of my high school baseball career came in my junior year when my high school baseball team won the state championship — the first in the school's history. This was an incredible accomplishment because the Fighting Seminoles had losing seasons the previous 10 years and finished last in our league the year before.

I felt like I was on top of the world. With this win, my focus turned to playing well my senior year and earning a college scholarship to a Division I school.

Things, however, did not turn out the way I had hoped my senior year. My high school team came within one out of going to the state championship tournament and no Division I school offered me a baseball scholarship.

I was invited to play in the Seminole County All-Star game. This, I thought, would be my chance to show I could play at the next level. Every kids' dream is to play at the next level, and I was ready to prove myself. That's when a high school coach told me that I'd never play major college baseball. That was hurtful, but not defeating. I didn't believe him. I was raised to believe in myself so I just kept playing hard and giving 100 percent.

My prom date, Heather Youman, and I smile for the camera. I wore a crown because my class voted me Prom King.

25

When it came time to pick a college, I followed in the Ecksteins' footsteps. Dad, Mom, Ken, Christine, and Susan all went to the University of Florida. So I became a Gator too.

The problem was the UF baseball coaches didn't know my name. So in August, before fall baseball tryouts, Christine went with me to meet the Florida baseball coaches. We asked about the tryout dates. I was pleased when the coaches offered to let me use the batting cages until the tryouts.

Every day I worked out in the cages on my own. I wasn't allowed on the field, where returning team members were running and playing catch on their own. When the official practice started, a second baseman suddenly transferred to another school. The Gators needed a backup second baseman for scrimmages. Because I was the only person who hit in the cages every day, the coaches invited me to scrimmage. They didn't give me a uniform, but I did get a hat. That was enough for me. I played my hardest and I made the team.

I did not play much my freshman year. However, in my sophomore year, I earned a position at second base and, later, a scholarship for my junior and senior years. Rick, who also played baseball, transferred to UF my junior year and made the team.

At that time, all five of us were UF students. To make ends meet, we lived together to save money for my parents, who supported us all through school. True to our upbringing, all money was pooled together. We even shared a car and had to work out pick-up and drop-off schedules. Once again the family had to work together in order to move forward.

During my college baseball career, I set five school records and made the All-America Academic Team. My favorite memory was making it to the College World Series® in Omaha, Nebraska, and playing in the semifinals with my brother Rick. Late in the game Rick was moved from left field to third base, and we turned a double play together — a classic Eckstein-to-Eckstein moment and one that I'll always cherish. The team finished third, which made us all very proud and thankful.

My Florida records included:

- Runs scored — 222
- Hits — 276
- Hit by pitch — 41
- Assists — 671
- Double plays — 142
- 23 career home runs ranked 7th all-time.

After my last game as a UF Gator, a few Major League teams called. Some promised to pick me in the baseball draft. Some thought I might be taken in the 10th through 15th rounds.

The Boston Red Sox picked me in the 19th round. About 500 players were picked ahead of me, but I was grateful that my name was called. I was excited to sign my first professional contract, which paid a $1,000 bonus. The scout who signed me said I would have to prove myself all over again (he told my dad I'd probably play a few years in the minors and make a good coach). But I was used to proving myself.

My first day in the Minor Leagues™ I was stopped at the gate. Shawn Smith, the Lowell Spinners' general manager, said:

"Excuse me, son, can I help you?"

"I'm a second baseman," I answered.

"Oh, I thought you were someone's little brother," he said.

People still say I look very young and that does not bother me at all. It is a reminder looks can be deceiving — it's what's on the inside that decides who a person is and what a person can accomplish. Shawn and I still laugh about our first introduction and have remained friends for many years now.

For the first four games in Class A League, I sat the bench waiting for my chance to play. When I got that chance I went after it 100 percent. As a result, I had a great season and the manager said I deserved the team's Most Valuable Player award.

Boston's upper management overruled and decided the award should go to their star draft pick. Following family rules, I did not pout. Although winning the MVP award would have been a great honor, it was not a necessary award for me to continue striving to be the best baseball player I could be.

Following Class A league, I moved through Boston's Minor League™ system with stops in four towns in four years. I enjoyed the Minor Leagues™, and I met some great friends along the way.

Although some aspects of being in the Minor Leagues™ were tough - like the 14-hour bus rides —it was nothing compared to what my brother and sisters had to deal with in coping with their kidney failure. And they did it with a positive attitude. So I never complained.

29

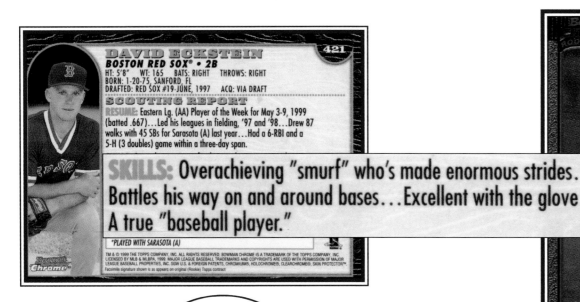

DAVID ECKSTEIN
BOSTON RED SOX® • 2B
421
HT: 5'8"   WT: 165   BATS: RIGHT   THROWS: RIGHT
BORN: 1-20-75, SANFORD, FL
DRAFTED: RED SOX #19-JUNE, 1997   ACQ: VIA DRAFT

SCOUTING REPORT
RESUME: Eastern Lg. (AA) Player of the Week for May 3-9, 1999 (batted .667)...Led his leagues in fielding, '97 and '98...Drew 87 walks with 45 SBs for Sarasota (A) last year...Had a 6-RBI and a 5-H (3 doubles) game within a three-day span.

SKILLS: Overachieving "smurf" who's made enormous strides... Battles his way on and around bases...Excellent with the glove... A true "baseball player."

*PLAYED WITH SARASOTA (A)

TM & © 1999 THE TOPPS COMPANY, INC. ALL RIGHTS RESERVED. BOWMAN CHROME IS A TRADEMARK OF THE TOPPS COMPANY, INC. LICENSED BY MLB & MLBPA, 1999. MAJOR LEAGUE BASEBALL TRADEMARKS AND COPYRIGHTS ARE USED WITH PERMISSION OF MAJOR LEAGUE BASEBALL PROPERTIES, INC. SGW U.S. & FOREIGN PATENTS. CHROMIUM®, HOLOCHROME®, CLEARCHROME®, SKIN PROTECTOR™. Facsimile signature shown is as appears on original (Rookie) Topps contract.

DAVID ECKSTEIN

My toughest experience in the minor leagues happened when I was on the AAA Red Sox team in Pawtucket, Rhode Island. The hitting instructors insisted I'd never play in the big leagues with my swing. So they changed it.

I tried hitting their way for 100 plate appearances —I really tried. But I had just nine hits in the 100 at-bats, and two were bunt hits. After every game I called home and talked about the game with my dad. I didn't tell my parents or family about the hitting change. I'm a pretty quiet guy and didn't want to complain. But my career was in free fall and I did not know what to do.

Finally, I told my family about what had happened.

The next day my brother Rick flew to Columbus, Ohio, to have a heart-to-heart talk with me. Because of the hitting adjustments, I had forgotten my old swing. Rick knew my swing and helped me get back to my old self.

After talking with Rick, I knew what I had to do. I apologized to the Boston coaches and said, "I need to do what I need to do for myself. I need to get back to being me." So I returned to hitting my way, and I began hitting the ball! By this time, it was too late. The Red Sox put me on waivers near the end of the season and it appeared my baseball career was over.

I talked with everyone in my family over the phone and they all encouraged me not to give up. "You can't quit now," they all said. "Someone will give you another chance."

Sure enough, that chance came thanks to the Anaheim Angels. The Angels picked me up and sent me to their Class AAA club in Edmonton for the final 15 games of the season. Having regained my old swing, I finished strong with a .346 batting average and three home runs. It earned me an invitation to Anaheim's 2001 spring training camp.

During camp, I heard the heartbreaking news that our family friend, Richard, died on the operating table. I felt a heavy heart, but was inspired at the same time as I knew Richard would always be there for me in spirit. Although Richard never played sports because of his medical problems, he would jokingly warn me, "You better play well, or I'll kick your butt." He always took an interest in my baseball career and would say, "I'll watch over you. Any coach I need to see? I'll get you a chance to play. The rest is up to you."

I would laugh at Richard when he said such things; however, in spirit, Richard must have whispered a few words to Anaheim Manager Mike Scioscia and Coach Alfredo Griffin because the strangest thing happened.

31

The Angels didn't need a second baseman for the 2001 season. They had Adam Kennedy. But an injury left a hole at shortstop. Somehow, the Angels' coaching staff decided that I should learn how to play shortstop while on the job, which doesn't happen much in the Major Leagues. I played shortstop only twice the previous two years and only 21 games in the Minor Leagues™. I knew this opportunity was a sign from Richard and my big chance to prove myself. Fortunately, during the offseason, I had practiced playing shortstop with my brother Rick, just in case something opened up.

Just before the first pitch of a spring game, I was sitting on the bench with the team, and Mr. Scioscia leaned over and said softly: "I just wanted to let you know you made the team." My heart wanted to burst with excitement. However, I kept my emotions to myself. As soon as I got back to my hotel I called my family with the great news: "I MADE THE TEAM!!!"

I've led the Majors in one category my first two years — being hit by a pitch. My first year I set a rookie record by being hit 21 times. Last year I was hit 27 times.

Now I was in the Major Leagues and I wanted to prove that I belonged. Dad always told us to walk into a room like you own the place. Not in an arrogant way, but with a quiet confidence. The difference between the two is the first you have to tell people how confident you are, and in the second, you show it by your actions.

Even though we finished 41 games out of first place in the AL West race in 2001, I felt we were on the doorstep of something great. We all knew we could improve if we kept a positive attitude. Having heart is easy when everything is going your way. The true test comes when things aren't going your way.

My game routines

- I eat pancakes for breakfast and chicken teriyaki pasta for lunch. After a game I'll have Frosted Flakes or Froot Loops. I can eat the same thing every day for months.
- I sprint on and off the field between innings.
- I sprint to first on a walk.
- In the on-deck circle, I whirl the bat around my shoulders and head to loosen my muscles and get mentally ready.

33

We opened the 2002 season with a 6-14 start, which was not good, to say the least. One thing that helped early on was a meeting Mr. Scioscia called during our first games in Seattle. He told us he believed in us. He said we had the talent to be champions, and I knew he was right.

Soon after, we started turning our season around by winning 21 of 24 games. We started to believe we could come from behind in any game. For the season we had 43 comeback wins. I even hit three grand slams, two on back-to-back days. Those were surprises since I never had hit a grand slam before.

AP/Wide World Photos

AP/Wide World Photos

34

As August slipped away, the Oakland A's won a record 20 games in a row. We kept our focus on what we could do and stayed in the race. Finally, we needed just one win to clinch a wild-card playoff spot. But we lost four straight days, giving the Seattle Mariners a chance to catch us.

Reporters reminded us that in 1995 the Angels blew an 11-game lead over Seattle in August and missed the playoffs. However, we were a different team, and what happened in the past was the past.

When we did beat the Texas Rangers to reach the playoffs, Scott Spiezio celebrated by picking me up and tossing me into a tub of ice water.

Ronald Martinez/Getty Images

AP/Wide World Photos

Even though our team lacked playoff experience, we supported each other, and knew we could win. Not even losing the first game of every series in the playoffs dampened our spirits. New York, the team with the most World Series® wins (26) and winner of four of the past six, was our first test. We passed the test. Next came the Minnesota Twins, where a three home run performance by Adam Kennedy in Game 5 propelled us to the World Series®.

Both series ended with me catching the final out. After the last game, I gave my dad both game-ending baseballs.

AP/Wide World Photos

36

Mom, Christine, Susan, Rick, and my nephew Kenny came to California for Games 6 and 7 of the World Series®. They all piled into my apartment, some sleeping on the floor in sleeping bags. This felt like home. Unfortunately, my dad, a Sanford city commissioner, could not come because he had important meetings to attend, but we spoke every day and he was with me in my heart.

During the World Series®, the anticipation of the games made me feel the most nervous. However, I felt fine once the games started. Despite all the excitement, my attention was focused on the game I had to play and what I needed to do to help my team.

The World Series® played out in perfect drama. Every pitch seemed to mean everything. Barry Bonds put on a gigantic display of power with four home runs. Our shining moment came in Game 6. People always ask me now if I gave up when our team was down 5-0 in the seventh? No I didn't. I knew we needed to make a move pretty soon. I kept thinking, "We have to find a way to get one run. The hardest thing is the first run."

Scott Spiezio's three-run homer gave us the lift we needed and a two-run double by Troy Glaus gave us the win.

I started off Game 7 with a rare baserunning mistake. I didn't get back to second base on a line-drive flyout. Despite my mistake, I knew that I had to put it behind me and stay focused on the present moment. By remaining focused and not letting my mistake affect my thinking, I hit a leadoff single in the third inning that started a three-run rally, capped by Garret Anderson's bases-loaded double. Neither team scored the rest of the game, and we won 4-1.

My most memorable moment about the post-game celebrations was having my family on the field with me after the game. We hugged with joyful sighs of relief while a wonderful sea of red fans waved and cheered with Halo Sticks. I'll always treasure that moment.

During the on-field celebrations, I called dad from my cell phone to share in the moment. I also called my high school baseball coach, Mike Powers, and thanked him for all he had done for me.

The offseason held a few surprises. I was invited to play on a Major League Baseball All-Star team that toured Japan. The team needed a bullpen catcher so I told them my brother, Rick, could do the job. They gave him a chance, and he joined us. Together, Rick and I had an amazing trip, and we both felt incredibly privileged to be among some of the best players in baseball today.

Also, in Japan, I got to see my first live on-screen glimpse of our Angel Rally Monkey™. Although a video of the Rally Monkey™ is played on the big screen at Edison Field to fire up the fans, I never looked at it during an Angel game. In fact, I never look at the scoreboard because I should know the score without looking. I also don't want to know my batting average or even talk about statistics during the season because it has the potential to take my focus from the game.

After returning home from Japan, I received an invitation from George Will to have dinner with President George W. Bush and other baseball people at the White House. I was able to bring one guest, so I brought my mom. She was thrilled. Not only did we have dinner with the President, we also had a tour of the White House by President Bush himself! It was an awesome experience and one we will never forget.

Brian Bahr/Getty Images

During the offseason, Angel teammates called me on the phone and said, "Are you working out right now? You better be!"

I can guarantee you that none of the Angels' players, or staff, is ready to take it easy because we won the World Series® in 2002. Success doesn't guarantee future success. You have to earn it each season.

For me to be successful, it starts with being prepared physically and mentally. I run, lift weights, practice fielding and hitting during the winter. Also, I get my mind focused on the game and thinking positively about the challenges that I must meet in the upcoming season.

AP/Wide World Photos

I realize that even the best prepared will face unexpected challenges. In fact, something unexpected has happened to my family again. Last year, my father was diagnosed with kidney failure. Although he is not on dialysis yet, he is going through the process of preparing for a kidney transplant.

There are many unanswered questions about my father's health; we, as a family, will help Dad in his fight for life, trusting in our faith and the skill of doctors.

My father's struggle, like the battle my siblings endured, is a reminder to me to cherish every moment and to persevere no matter what. That is why I play so hard. It is what having heart is all about.

It means that no matter what happens — no matter what curveball life may throw you — you never lose faith, you never lose respect for yourself or others, and you never lose the belief that every second of your life is worth giving the best that you can. It's all about having heart.

Stephen Dunn/Getty Images